DANIEL SILVER

HEADS

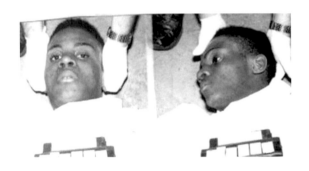

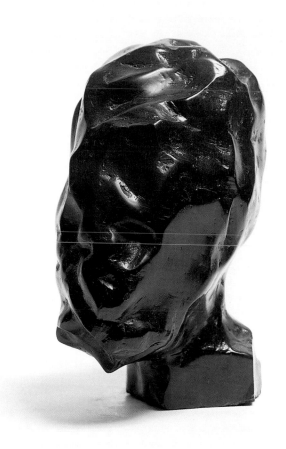

58

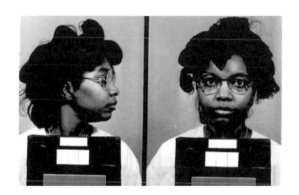

Daniel Silver's studio, London, 2006

DEMOS

Alistair Robinson

Daniel Silver's new body of work, *Demos*, continues his longstanding preoccupation with creating new ways to remake what is arguably the oldest and most traditional type of artform – the three-dimensional, free-standing figure. Silver's practice is based in expanding the vocabulary of 'sculpture' into new territory, whilst continuing a dialogue with both the history of modern art and the wider story of Western art.

Demos has marked several departures for the artist, in terms of subject matter, process, and materials. In previous projects, Silver has worked with what might loosely be described as 'figure studies' – quasi-abstract forms created from the figure or head but with their own formal logic. But in *Demos* the artist has restricted himself to the portrait bust as a format. More importantly, in *Demos*, each object 'stands in' for a particular individual, or at least was made with reference to a particular person. In previous works, Silver has selected his motifs in part to provide an opportunity for sculptural experimentation - for adventures in creating new form from inert matter. Here, each of the heads was carved with reference to historical individuals – specifically, of police portrait photographs of individuals on death row in America. Silver's figures remain anonymous, rather than being memorialised or sentimentalised – but they represent a class of people, largely African-American, who are without a voice or a means to represent themselves. In *Demos* the artist's intention is not that his works are read as illustrations of a political argument. Whilst engaging with a contentious political issue, his subject matter, working method and form are interlocked. Silver's modus operandi deliberately complicates the relationship between the form of an artwork and the creator's ideas, process and identity. His way of working in creating *Demos* has been to work with a team of collaborators in Zimbabwe - highly skilled African sculptors able to adapt their own tradition rather than operating merely as fabricators.

This process has developed from Silver's interest in the history of modern art – as he has remarked, "modernist sculpture always goes back to Africa. But instead of looking at work 'about' African sculpture, I wanted to be there". Even though Silver has a longstanding connection with Zimbabwe, being of (white) Zimbabwean and South African parentage, his project has risks attached. How to avoid a kind of colonial relationship to another tradition of art production, is one obvious problem. Silver's solution to the issue of appropriating other artists' formal characteristics (or indeed their labour) has been to work with the team of Zimbabwean artists to allow them to experiment, within his specified parameters, and to work on each object together. Accordingly it is impossible to discern which works in the project bear the marks of his hand, and which were undertaken or completed by his collaborators. Instead of creating an ironic take on previous artists' appropriation of African art, Silver arrives at a genuine intertwining of different traditions. One of his aims remains akin to that of his modernist predecessors, i.e. to create objects which speak not in a polite voice, but with an expressive force; and whose presence is due to their formal properties rather than their naturalism.

Silver's choices of material and method in *Demos* have been determined by several connected factors. One of these has been the desire to find specific types of stone - namely black springstone and bottle-green soapstone, both of which are widely available in Zimbabwe. A second has been the desire to work with artists greatly skilled in stone carving. And a third is the artist's fascination with modernists' preference for direct carving, popularised by Henry Moore, amongst others, in the 1920s. Silver's works, as suggested above, reprise some of the forms and processes of modernist sculpture to critique the assumptions and ideologies associated with them. Direct carving might best be interpreted as a modernist-romantic commitment to authenticity of individual expression and as part of a commitment to 'truth to materials'. It is, now, associated with what a century ago would have been called 'primitivist' ideas of immediacy and vitality of expression. *Demos* asks which of these ideas are still potent, and which anachronistic.

Silver's work has until now resembled earlier artists' development of an abstraction rooted in the figure, relying on our propensity to 'read in' the forms of heads and bodies from the most minimal or even unlikely cues. Accordingly his works are best read, initially, in terms of their formal properties – their rhythm of void and solid, convex and concave plane, and their relation to the qualities of their materials. Any viewer with a familiarity with the history of sculpture is likely to register the work as either a critique or a continuation of the moderist figurative tradition. Indeed Silver is best seen as celebrating that tradition, lightening it with humour and deepening it with new method and subject matter. Of special interest to Silver are those artists of the last quarter of the 19th century and the first quarter of the 20th whose work liberated the representation of the figure in three dimensions.

At times, the artist's works recall those of Rodin and Medardo Rosso - often he will present fragments of bodies, or cut-up figures which seem to spring to life from out of surrounding abstract passages of modelling or carving. On other occasions, his work makes reference to the heavily, even crudely modelled forms pioneered by Matisse and Picasso in the 1900s, and their inspiration in what were then imagined to be 'primitive' cultures. Other works can possess a mask-like blankness, redolent of Henri Gaudier-Brzeska's bronzes or early Jacob Epstein, both seminal figures in the British sculptural tradition and indebted to African art. Crucially, although concerned with reanimating early modernist ideas and forms, Silver is equally indebted to figures such as Franz West, whose seriousness of intent is matched by an ebullient, provocative sense of humour. Silver's forms, in their brutal urgency and black comedy, are unmistakably contemporary.

The artist's relationship to canonical European artists can be illustrated through a couple of contrasting examples. The work on page 48, is chiselled into hundreds of fragmented, irregular planes, as though a cubist-primitivist portrait. In particular, it resembles Picasso's 'Head of a Woman' of 1909, made when he encountered African sculpture and remarked "my greatest artistic emotions were aroused [by] the sublime beauty of the sculptures created by anonymous artists in Africa". In Silver's work, the features of the figures feel as if they have become animated or are dissolving into liquid form. The spectator is required to imaginatively synthesise multiple impressions – only after slow and comprehensive registration of each facet can we arrive at an 'image' of the work, so that irresolute form can become resolved into a legible unity. Encountering the work for the first time, it feels as though the object is ebbing and flowing away from our grasp. Silver makes our eye dart from point to point across the object's surface in order to arrive at a complete picture of the whole.

The work on page 27, by contrast, is characterised by asymmetry, frontality, and hugely simplified planes – the transitions between which are angular, even jagged. Unlike the above work, here Silver's formal decisions recall Gaudier's, and the latter's "concentration of energy, compression of mass [and] vitalistic density", in Benjamin Buchloh's phrase. A similar sense of contained energy, even brutality, is expressed by Silver through almost geometric volumes and sharp angularity. This work appears to have lost all of its extremities, and has a startling lack of resolution around the areas which define character in a traditional portrait, namely the eyes and mouth. As with early modernist sculpture, our attention is deflected from the conventional signifiers of expression onto the form of the object as a whole, and its configurations of volume and mass. Even more than with other works in *Demos*, this piece gives the initial impression of being 'unfinished', excessively awkward and asymmetrical, and with the figure's features all but illegible. But a second glance reveals that the work has a pristine high polish, indicating that hours of labour have been invested in its 'finish'. Moreover, the linear marks in the subject's hair and forehead are crisply defined, delicate and sinuous, in contrast to the craggy forms around the mouth and ears.

The combination of apparently contradictory registers – of grace and grave brutality – throws into question how we should read the object. Silver leaves it entirely open how far we should relate such brittle, dislocated forms to the violence associated with both 'subject' and the 'process' – Zimbabwe having a contested, indeed tragic recent history. Silver also leaves it open as to how far his use of indeterminacy is intended to be an echo of the traditional modernist device of presenting a sculpture as though in the process 'of becoming'. In both Medardo Rosso and Rodin's works, we are given the impression that animate form is emerging from within lumpen wax, bronze or stone, driven by the life-force within it. However, in Silver's works we might be more likely to feel that the individual's characteristics are in the process of erasure rather than in genesis. It is as though the individual's subjectivity - registered by their unique combination of features – is being lost to history. Indeed certain objects in *Demos* resemble medieval British figure carvings, truncated by the violence of the Reformation then left to erode slowly through exposure to pollution and acid rain. We might imagine the work on page 27 having once possessed delicately articulated features, now flattened into a residual single plane over time. It feels as though the subject's eye-sockets have been hollowed out and smoothed away by natural forces, over decades or centuries.

Characterisation, in Silver's sculptures, might best be described as transferred onto a different plane - his intention is not to prevent the viewer empathising and identifying with the unnamed subject, but to defer it. His works' power comes, in part, from the impression that history, and wider forces, have overwhelmed, indeed subsumed each represented individual, of whom only the kernel remains visible to the world. The indistinctness of their features might well be seen to reflect the fact that their willpower is a disruptive force that the wider body politic sees fit to extinguish. Encountering *Demos*, our role is to imaginatively conjure an individual's presence from the traces of likeness which still remain. Our eye is invited to wander around each area of the sculpture, rather than be detained by characterisation or narrative, so that the formal properties and thematic content sit in a tense equilibrium. *Demos* might, therefore, be viewed as akin to a history painting (the phrase 'history sculpture' having no currency) rather than a set of portraits.

Silver has described how he intends each head to be encountered as a "witness" more than a mere portrait. Rather than be read as a second-hand representation of another object in the world, their role is to emanate what Walter Benjamin calls artworks' "palpable knowledge". For Silver, the best portraits "embody" both the presence of a sentient being and abstract ideas. His intention is for his objects to act as both emblems of their time and to carry a vital psychological charge. The artist sees his work as presenting something more akin to a first-hand testimony of its time rather than a likeness; verisimilitude is not the aim. As Silver remarks, "the figures are witnesses - they all know that something has happened, and have a collective knowledge or memory. They seem to share this with us, but feel to be withholding it at the same time. I feel they know something. What do they know?". The artist's decision to restrict himself to the bust-portrait is closely related to his subject matter. As historian Tristram Hunt has recently argued, the Enlightenment's "proliferation of the sculpted portrait... celebrated a typically politicised sense of civic virtue". Hunt has noted that the cult of the portrait and bust marked the true emergence of "civil society", and that "advances in portraiture occurred alongside intellectual movements similarly given to stress human potential". Silver's advanced style allows him to explore the relationships between sculpture and 'civil society' in both the West and the 'developing' world.

Working in series has also enabled the artist to bring into being an entire landscape of figures: *Demos* consists of over 100 heads. Throughout his career, Silver has been interested in the presentation mechanisms and display devices associated with both historical and modern sculpture - from plinths, cases and platforms to the idea of the museum as a medium of display. His works to date have rested on specially constructed chairs, tables, boxes, castors, and shelves, or been (literally) housed in room-scale constructions. Silver calls these "homes for sculpture"; they are a means of framing and presenting objects to our attention, whilst being integral to his practice. Previously, Silver has painted plinths and whole rooms in tertiary colours and candy shades - from cyan, lime green and acid-pink to clay red or mustard yellow. Such colours amplify his works' combination of charm and threat, of intensity of feeling and off-beam wit.

Demos, though, has seen a further departure. Each object is presented atop a simple, rectilinear plinth, painted in either low-toned, muted, chalky colours redolent of period properties or high-key pinks and oranges. Their contrasting presence in the gallery creates quite different points of orientation for the viewer: Silver's presentation becomes more akin to museums' orchestrations of classical fragments or collections of baroque busts. Their appearance as time-worn fragments amplifies this effect. Encountering *Demos* as a whole is to immerse oneself in what Silver calls a "silent crowd" - to be surrounded by an image of modern life. Spread across the gallery, the objects feel close to a mass presence, hence the collective title of the work - the Greek for 'entire populace'. Scanning across them in an exhibition context, the viewer is confronted by a sense of inhabiting a city-in-miniature with its own population; when in the centre of the work he or she is engulfed into a forest of columnar forms.

Alistair Robinson is Programme Director of Northern
Gallery for Contemporary Art, Sunderland, and
has held curatorial positions at the National Museum
of Photography, the Victoria & Albert Museum
and The Lowry.

'Demos', Northern Gallery for Contemporary Art, 2007

DRAWINGS

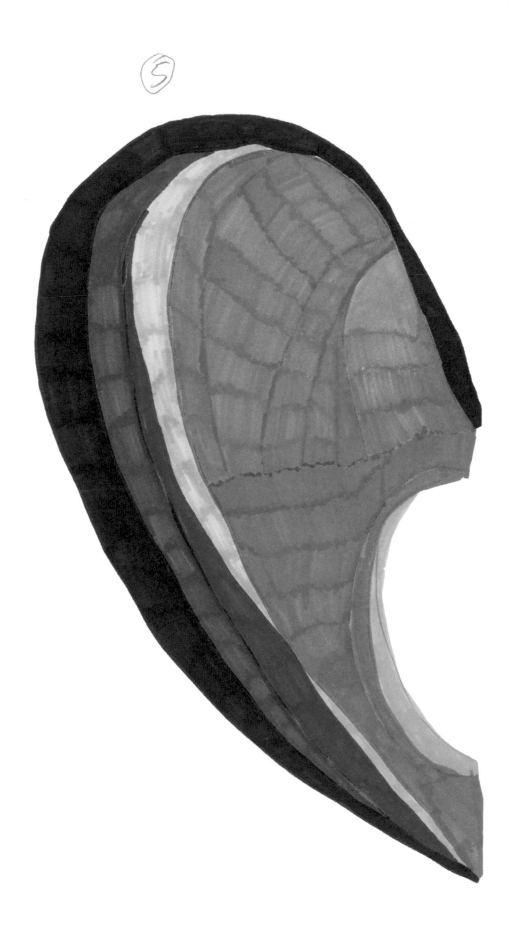

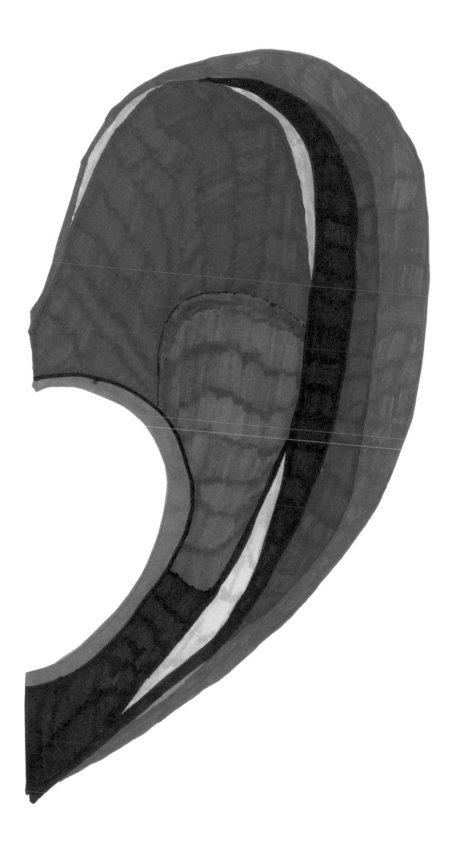

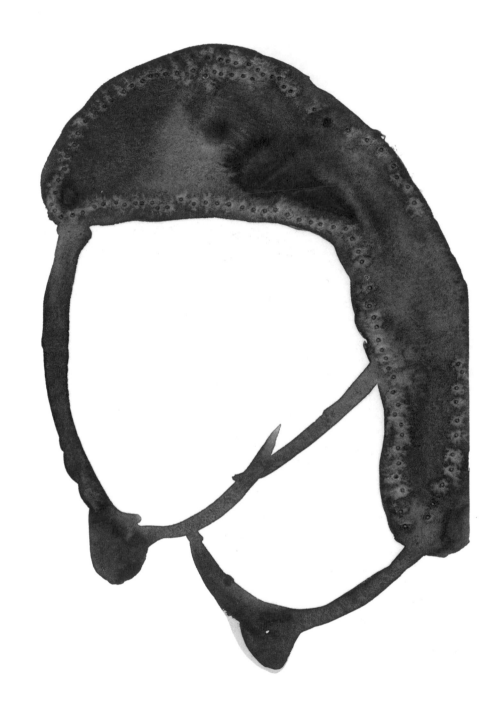

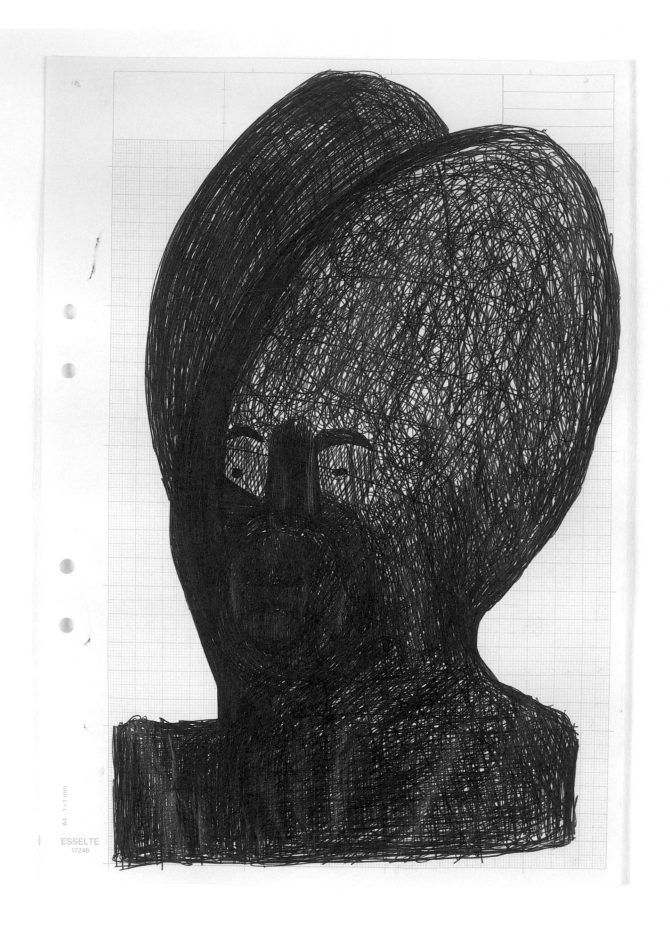

ESSELTE
17246

A4 - 1×1 mm

THE DYSLEXIC SCULPTURE OF DANIEL SILVER

Paulo Herkenhoff

Daniel Silver's sculpture is a 'dyslexic' body. It can also be a 'dyslexic' physical complex, that some might call installation. That is the departure point for knowledge. The 'dyslexic sculpture' refuses to follow a canon, or an established grammar which builds meanings, or work in pre-mapped territory. It takes risks. Like Constantin Brancusi's anatomical disparities, juxtaposition of cultural references, and conjugation of unlikely materials, Silver's sculpture creates a poetic semantics appropriate to a fractured world. Brancusi harmonized heterogeneous materials, yet kept the integrity of sculpture. For Silver too, harmony lies outside the tyranny of formal signifiers.

1. In conversation with the author on March 5, 2007.

Silver says, "I made the sculptures; and then I needed a place to put them so would construct a whole place for them".[1] This empirical question – the artist's need for a 'place' for his sculptures – takes Silver to territory similar to Brancusi's, and to the issue of the plinth. In Silver's case, one object can be finished and complete, like *Page: go there, just there,* (see p98) - a anthropomorphic object that assembles a spinning wig on top of electric appliances or *Woman in the Mountain: Woman on the Mountain, Head in the Mountain* (see p106). Yet the artist keeps inventing a 'lack', a need to expand the field of the object. The 'dyslexic sculpture' needs to suppress this demand; to learn its presence in the world. As a consequence, a work can be simultaneously the object (a study in mass and volume); the object and its supporting devices (plinths, platforms, shelves, furniture, cubicles, and others); or else the entire space where both are articulated and brought to life by the presence of the viewer. Thus *Page: go there, just there* is both an autonomous object as well as a component of the installation *Page: go there, just there.*

Thus, in the constructed environment of *The Buddha and the Chaise Longue* (see p100), we also find a shelf on which Silver places a collection of smaller sculptures. It is a small exposition of "quick sculptures", within a larger context. The incorporation of a room of the gallery into the work has the function of providing a space for thought. Plinths may be painted in vivid colors to produce the visual articulation of *Winning the Cornetto,* (see p96), In the *Cake Snake* (see p94) show in Rome, of 2001, Silver ordered space through clusters of dialogues. The *Cake Snake* itself was a conversation piece of five objects. Two sculptures (a head and chair) proposed a dialogue or a silence depending on how the head was positioned towards the viewer. This methodology results in installations with entities (parts) which contribute with specific meanings for a both visual and conceptual discourse. Now, the viewer is contextualized in this imaginary dialogue. Silver's installations are like the setting of schizophrenic architecture of anxiety to belong and to integrate splittered emotions. There is no sublimation, horror is contained.

Some of Silver's sculptures are adverbs without being a place, like *Woman in the Mountain, Woman on the Mountain, Head in the Mountain*, which incorporates the legs of a cheap African sculpture. No matter how cheap, the piece deals with cultural contamination, a culture within another, inscribed in the structure of another. Others are visual adverbs, like the head sitting on a chair and the monkey on *The Buddha and the Chaise Longue*. The 'dyslexic sculptures' establish new symbolic layers to the adverbs. Viewers are not there to be passive onlookers. Silver places them inside the emotional fabric of the works. Part of their responsibility is bringing Silver's projects either into a unique cohesive experience, or to maintain its fragmentation.

What is a sculpture for Daniel Silver?

His answer depends on, and relates to each work. Since the sculptor and this author met at a salon in Louise Bourgeois's house in New York in February 2006, Bourgeois will be purposely quoted throughout this text, in reference to issues raised around the sculpture of Daniel Silver. Since his oeuvre is irreducible to a signature image, this text deliberately runs as a fractured essay.

The work of Daniel Silver is built about embodying memories and the process of sculpting history. Louise Bourgeois, who is a collector since childhood, uses her garments, spanning eight decades of existence, in her installation 'Cell (Clothes)', 1996 to confine memories. "I travel in time, not in space," she says. Franz Ackerman travels in geography to make paintings with a touristic memory, acting as a modern flâneur. Silver travels through exhibitions, creating their own environment as part of the work, or incorporating museographic remnants of past shows. All the heads in *Daniel Silver at Pescali & Sprovieri* (see p102), the title for show at the Pescali & Sprovieri Gallery, London, incorporated bases made with the waste of the installation of a Henry Moore exhibition at the Dulwich Picture Gallery, 2004. In fact this is Silver's critical cannibalization of the museum as social memory, in the process in which museums themselves are seen as cannibal machines.[2]

The heads of the installation *Daniel Silver at Pescali & Sprovieri* were a reference to the form of location of bust-portraits by Bernini and other

2. See Donald Preziosi, 'The Art of Art History'. Oxford, Oxford University Press, 1998, pp. 507-525.

3. In 2005, Sacha Craddock has made a detailed analyses of the exhibition in the text *Hindsight* and raises the *United Colors of Benetton* issue.

4. Ronald Segal, Daniel Silver's great-uncle, wrote 'The Black Diaspora', Faber & Faber, London, 1995 / Farrar, Straus, Giroux, New York, 1995

5. See the interview 'Creator in the Hands of Matter'. Nana Portal, March 14, 2006.

6. In conversatation with Paulo Herkenhoff in New York, October 26-28, 2006. All unidentified quotes by Daniel Silver came from these conversations.

7. *Presenting Daniel Silver* in *The Buddha and the Chaise Longue*, text by Stephen V. Wilson.

sculptors and the architects in Rome. Daniel Silver operates with a sense of historicity, between Bernini and Benetton.[3] 'Heads' had to be done in Zimbabwe with local people. It is not arbirtrary. His mother grew up in Rhodesia, the present Zimbabwe. Thus, this dislocation is also doing sculpture under the Jewish Diaspora and within an international dialogue. A relative of Silver's wrote a history of the black diaspora.[4] "I'm from here and there, yet still I'm neither from here nor there," Silver told Eitan Buganim in respect to his double nationality, English and Israeli.[5] It is a sort of "material history". *Untitled (Man with Wings)* (see p105) is a male totemic figure made of different African and European woods, chosen both for their organic and plastic qualities and their geographic origins. "African sculptures are like the autistic children I have to look after," Silver realizes.[6] For Stephen V. Wilson, the furniture of *The Buddha and the Chaise Longue* provides "a safe place to negotiate an event or witness a psychic error."[7] The installation confronts the viewer with many cartographic connections. It confronts the East / West ethics of meditation and leisure. The monkey stands for the oriental wisdom of detachment from the world (not seeing, not hearing, not speaking) and for the Western caricature of human limitations, like in the 17th century northern painting. In both cases, it represents the mind uncontrolled, emotional.

Our gaze can understand the status of Silver's sculpture only if accepting to wander in his erratic itinerary. Silver portrays the brutality of Western ethical deviations: racial profiling, racisms, reductionist ideas on primitivism, colonialism as social cannibalism, the internal incorporation of oppressive values in Africa (Franz Fanon). Oppression is asymmetrical.

Heads.

For Daniel Silver, a sculpture, like a beard, is something that grows in your body if you belong to a certain biological category (male), or an ideological category (man). Or it may grow within one. Or be a significant investment by the viewer in the work. Some sculptures might look like toys, but they can only be a perverse reversion of aspects of their symbolic games.

The fragmented body from modernity – from Théodor Géricault's *Têtes Coupées*, 1818-1819, to Ernesto Neto and Damien Hirst, via *The Destruction of the Father*, 1974, by Louise Bourgeois – is a body without organs; a desiring machine; a machine célibataire; an erotic motor; a found object; a ready made. It can also be the hysterical body. Silver's work is the embodiment of states of "being-in-the-world". It is a body with good humour or deep melancholy. It is the body of the adolescent, of the Oedipal mother, of a politician, or a body sculpted by social abandonment.

For Silver, a sculpture is a body that is ruled by an etiology. It is emotion contained. Sculpture gives tangibility to the states of stress that Silver wishes to make legible. He enjoys the work of Marlene Dumas: "What I like about her work is that you look at it and it looks back at you, and it looks real". Her watercolors seem like symptoms exuded as internal pain. Silver's work operates pathological extraction and construction. They are unidealized states of being-in-the world.

When Silver says: "I am not interested in the body. I am interested in the head. A head can become more of an object than a body, because you can handle it like a football," he means it from the sculptural point of view. Heads inhabit his installations, always playing a crucial role as a desiring machine: the oedipal personage-sculpture *Mom, is that your lover?* (see p95), and the hysteric movement of *Page: go there, just there*. The psychic mechanics in Silver's oeuvre flows between Deleuze and Guattari's anti-Oedipus in *Mom, is that your lover?*s' schizophrenic role, and Breuer and Freud (Studies in Hysteria) in the obsessive disorder of *Page: go there, just there*. "The reason I make the heads is, on the one hand to continue the bust-making tradition, and on the other that they are the most interesting part of the body, the most object-like part of the body".

Making a good sculpture results in two physical reactions in the sculptor. The sculpture becomes a symptom.

"At one moment, I feel like going to the toilet to take a wee and at the same time I am very thirsty and wanting to drink... I always relate the urine and the thirst to my father being a nephrologist... He was always telling us to check the color of our urine and if we had drunk enough water... My father always said that van Gogh went mad because of the fumes of the turpentine that you get with oil painting... I don't know if this has to do with the embodiment in my work". (see p80)

In Daniel Silver's body of work, watercolours and drawings are perforated bodies. They are thought sculpturally. They are active elements, not only visual decorative outlining. Perforations are inscribed in the paper (the body). In their perforations and translucency, they breath like skin. Silver's drawings however, compared to his sculptures, could be thought as more mental operations.

Art history.

Daniel Silver operates with a sense of social and aesthetic perversion like Damien Hirst, the Chapman Brothers or Marc Quinn. Silver knows they did not invent aesthetic perversion in British art, but they rather took it to unexpected spheres. Quinn's *Cybernetically Engineered – Cloned and Grown Rabbit*, 2004 is an invented being that results in an uncanny spirit, like the dictator in Silver's *A Retreat for Rogue Leaders* (see p97). This is a monument to corruption and decadence. The impressive dictator has a Mexican sombrero and is covered with muesli (an allusion to the protection given by the Swiss bank system to money made from corruption). At the Retreat, the dictator enjoys life. The exiled dictator is part of the contemporary urban entropy: he lives in a shack-installation in a formerly

8. This is the account by
the artist on March 4, 2007.

pristine Gropius planning in Berlin.[8] The viewer is an impotent voyeur of
the criminal, as the scene can only be observed from the outside through
small window-holes.

In previous generations, Daniel Silver likes Antony Gormley and Eduardo
Paolozzi. Gormley's human figures are engaged in spiritual acts. They
proliferate – in this sense 'Heads' are also a proliferation – and symbolize
the material culture of different parts of the world. Paolozzi takes the
constructive and concretist traditions of European art to create machine-
bodies. Visually, some individuals in the sculptures of Daniel Silver seem
to be in the verge of dissolving or collapsing under their clumsy structure
or their abject flesh, melting like expanded foam. By opposition, the psychic expenditure of the small portraits by Francis Bacon (Henrietta
Moraes or George Dyer) resonates in the intensely absenteist emotions –
almost imperceptible – of some of Silver's individuals. Bacon "est un
criminel avoué" ("Bacon is an avowed criminal"), argues Phillipe Sollers.[9]
So is Silver's dictator. Some 'Heads' are "criminels avoués". Louise Bourgeois thinks that Bacon painted with adrenaline rush on the nervous
system brought on by the obsessive need to express himself, his
uncontrollable rage and desire: "Bacon's emotions may not have been
murderous, but they were certainly violent. He is a painter of terrific
brutality. It is a violence that is inflicted on the other and on the self".[10]
Silver inherits that "terrific brutality" and blends it with caustic sense
of humour.

9. L'Expérience Intérieure de
Francis Bacon. L'Infini, Paris,
Gallimard, n.3, Autumn 1990,
p.38.

10. Francis Bacon in Francis
Bacon. Paris, Galerie Lelong,
1999, p.47.

The origin of Silver's violentation of form goes even further back in time
references. It is to be discerned within the history of British sculpture
of the twentieth century. It is in Gaudier-Brzeska's forms and theory.
According to Ezra Pound, "the modern sculptor is a man who works with
instincts... his sculpture has no relation to classic Greek, but is continuing
the tradition of barbaric people of the earth (for whom we have sympathy
ad admiration)" according to Ezra Pound.[11] We need to return to the
ideas of "sympathy and admiration". Silver quotes Epstein and especially
Gaudier-Brzeska. Some of his sculptures, like *Woman on the Mountain,
Woman in the Mountain, Head in the Mountain* and *Untitled (Man with
Wings)*, are akin to the awkward narrative continuity and structure of
Epstein's *Venus* of 1913.

11. Gaudier-Brzeska
London, Jones Lane, 1916,
p.35. Reprinted.

The work of Silver quotes an extensive history of sculpture, not only
Bernini. The delicate pathos of Medardo Rosso's sculptures becomes a
eschatological material in *Mom, is that your lover?*. Emotions, which exude
in elegant containment in the figures by Rosso, are blind here. Silver
proves that the malleability of wax is not only to "express", but also to
constitute silence and censorship. His understanding of the plurality of
tasks of wax in his sculpture resonates with observations by Louise Bourgeois: "We are as malleable as wax. As a consequence, we are as sensible
to memories of what has happened before and the apprehension of what is
going to happen".[12] In the 'Cake Snake' show of 2001, a half-length
figure, with his legs formed by a table, alludes to the structure of Alberto

12. Conversation with
Paulo Herkenhoff on July 21, 2000.

Giacometti. It cannot have the anguish of the post-war Giacometti, but its silence and blind gaze does bring much of the sense of loss and mute perplexity of this century. On the floor group, the central figure is half toys and half reference to Claes Oldenburg early sculptures. Structurally, *Cake Snake* also has much of the symbolist assemblage of *Female Torso With Coiled Snake*, 1895-1905, by Rodin.

In 'Daniel Silver at Pescali & Sprovieri', Daniel Silver discussed the Roman statuary. All heads rest on table-like plinths. They are discretely disembalanced. The overpopulation of heads denotes how Silver has observed the amount of heads and busts in monuments and museums. Bernini under the patronage of Pope Urban VIII was the uttermost model. In 'Daniel Silver at Pescali & Sprovieri', the gaze of the heads installs a sort of a dyslexic dialogue with history. Some of the heads are models from the National Portrait Gallery, London. This makes it an intriguing conversation piece in which dyslexia, aphasia, silence and alienation are the grain of the discourse.

"Humanity is male and man defines woman not in herself but as relative to him; she is not regarded as an autonomous being," says Simone de Beauvoir, the author of 'The Second Sex', 1949. Would then de Beauvoir, the revolutionary writer on the female condition, call Silver's *The Three Wisemen* 'first sex' sculptures? He represents a paternal order with the heads of the painter Monet, the scientist Darwin, and a religious man. The three men configure three realms of knowledge. The use of bronze to cast the beards, instead of malleable and breakable materials (wax, terracotta, expandable foam, soapstone), points to the solidity of this structure of power through knowledge, an issue for Foucault. The counterpart to this male order comes again from de Beauvoir: "One is not born, but rather becomes, a woman." Hence, one is not born, but rather becomes, a man; but one also becomes a hysterical man (Charcot, Freud, and Louise Bourgeois); a criminal (in spite of Lombroso); a wise man; a bearded man; or a sculpture (Daniel Silver). Sacha Craddock raises that the wise men could also be John Ruskin, Pierre-Auguste Renoir, Auguste Rodin or August Sander. One can be displaced from Silver's trilogy of the wise men to the condition of criminals in his multitude of 'Heads'. Then, a double racial profiling would occur. His Darwin can no longer explain neither the origin of species nor the origin of colonial prejudice. "Now every man that has a beard is stopped by the police because he could be a religious leader, a Muslim," says Silver commenting on the post September 11 racial profiling of Muslims.

'Demos'

The *Demos* are a proliferation of heads, an excess of busts like in the Roman monuments or in African contemporary diaspora. Daniel Silver went to the internet for "mug shots" photos. "I really chose them because they are very sculptural images." All the heads have a photographic soul that could portray contemporary stress. For Daniel Silver, the fabric of the

13. Propero & Caliban. Trad. Pamela Powesland. Ann Harbor, The University of Michigan Press, 1990.

14. Some images were searched by the artist in the Google under "Death Roll Texas".

15. Translated Alan Sheridan. New York, Vintage Book, 1977.

Demos brings him back to his family history. "Mother lived in Rhodesia in the 'fifties and left in 1965." *Demos* is a return to the origin of the artist. It corresponds to a passage in the artist's family in the Jewish Diaspora. Actually, his mother was born in Bulawayo, in the present Zimbabwe, the former Rhodesia. Silver traveled to a village near Harare in Zimbabwe to work with local carvers. The social contract and aesthetics involved in creating *Demos* touches on the idea which Octave Mannoni outlines that the failure of colonization has a counterpart in feelings of abandonment and betrayal in former colonies.[13]

They are *Demos* in a Sartrean hell: "l'Enfer sont les autres" ("Hell are the others"), from a girl raped by a dog in Africa to convicts in the prison system in Texas. Some *Demos* come from the agonistic register of the death roll.[14] Some *Demos* are convicts: Texas Ex 946, Texas 999181, Texas Ex 700 1981... There is a disproportionally high number of Afro-Americans in the death roll. Silver here works on this form of racial profiling in criminology. Symbolically, they could be the same Texan prisoners singing in their forced labour in Nadine Robinson's installation 'Tower Hollers', 1999-2002. The *Demos* proliferate: besides the prisoners there are other characters: the beautified girl with dreadlocks and the agonic raped girl also, that touches the AIDS epidemic and the cultural imaginary about its forms of transmission in Africa. The head of the figure *Woman with Glasses* (see p62) lies on the uncomfortable surface in a similar position to the serene stability of Brancusi's 'Newborn' or the 'Sleeping Muse'. The idealized vulnerability, beauty and repose of Brancusi now lies unrestful as *Woman with Glasses*.

No-one is interested in being ethnocentric after the critical response to MoMA's exhibition 'Primitivism in Twentieth Century Art' of 1984 and mainly after Claude Lévi-Strauss's 'Race and History', when the art of the then called "primitives" was emancipated from the derogatory vision of the evolutionists, supported by social positivist theories and cultural Darwinism. In Silver's *Three Wise Man* (see p104), Darwin's head equals the religious man's, who can now be profiled as a 'barbarian' under contemporary prejudices. Silver deals with ethical zombies invented by sectarianism.

Silver's construction of a semiotics of punishment means an inflection towards Michel Foucault and his 'Discipline & Punish'.[15] The sculptures are inserted in an order that is immediately questioned. Some of the heads in *Demos* are related to the ethics and morbidity of Andy Warhol's *Electric Chair* and Louise Bourgeois's *Passage Dangereux*. They stand against death penalty. There is an intense differentiation within the repetition of the *Demos*: in spite of their extreme similarity there is individuality and disparity. As a group of heads, the *Demos* neither aim at totalization nor at a taxonomic system of organization. The first appearance of these soft stone bodies seems to have an excessively tactile surface. Skin and flesh are are as sensuously touched as by Degas, Picasso or Matisse. They are "docile bodies", as Foucault's concept has it.

An exhibition of Silver may recall the profusion of marble heads in Roman classic statuary. In *Demos*, there are diffuse states of rage, consciousness, agony, despair, emotional detachment, defense, abandonment. They are neither suicides nor moribund; they are doppelgangers, not the codified "Other" of Eurocentrism or capital. Punishment is already transferred from the body into the soul and from the soul onto the body. The *Demos* stand on long pedestals – an index of the phallic order. We cannot grasp their identity – if there is any – since any concept of who they are is dissolved. Guilt and innocence, fingerprints and chiseling, verdicts and representation, criminal identification and the portraiture – everything is mute and dead under the fantasmatic brutality of these heads. The tyranny of the signifier is dissolved. The Texan *Demos* has something of the pre-revolutionary France ritual of public exhibition of the convicts before their execution. In the Ancien régime, that exposure of the body of the condemned meant the exemplifying exhibition of the crime / criminal under Justice. "The image of the people in the death roll stuck in my memory," says Silver. Reversely in *Demos*, it stands for the modern State machine brutality and cybernetic exposure.

16. See Sarah Nuttat (editor). Beauty / ugly: African and diaspora aesthetics. Durham, Duke University Press, 2006.

For his work in Zimbabwe in 2006, he took an album of Texan prisoners on the death roll. The personal involvement of the artist and the labour-intensive production of the *Demos* are also oriented by a political discontent and disapproval. The work is not so much a European / African confrontation of ideals on beauty,[16] but it inflicts a brutality that is a crude call against the subtleties of western barbarianism. This is the ethics of the dyslexic sculpture within a double Diaspora complex (Africans and Jews). I am dyslexic and that is my very potentiality to take a shape of the world as a critical imagery construction. Before they are executed, the prisoners – could be one of the *Demos* – can choose their last meal and last words. One convict said: "I am an African warrior, born to breathe and born to die". For Silver, the Afro-American is indicating his pride for the origin and racial profiling of crime. "You brought me here to be executed, not to make a speech. That is it," said another. "It is also a good way to put art. You execute a sculpture," observers Daniel Silver.

Paulo Herkenhoff is an independent curator living in Rio de Janeiro. He is a former adjunct curator at the Museum of Modern Art in New York and artistic director of the XXIV Bienal de São Paulo (1998).

SELECTED WORKS
2001-2006

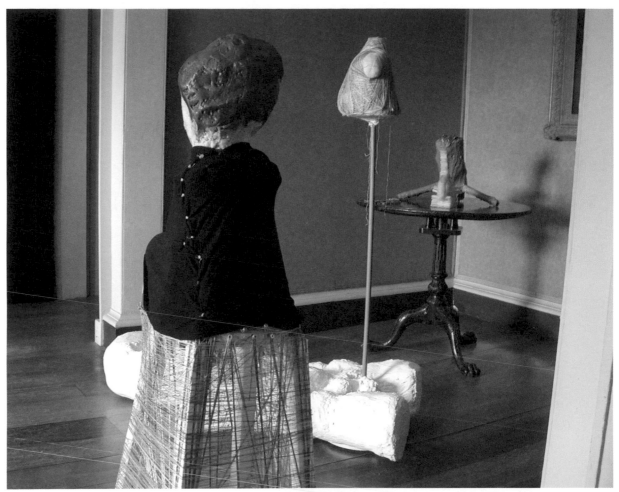

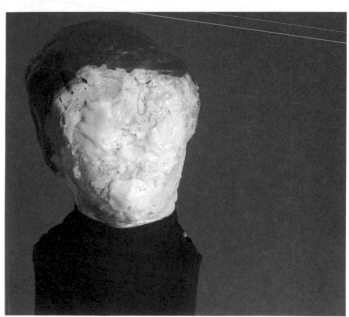

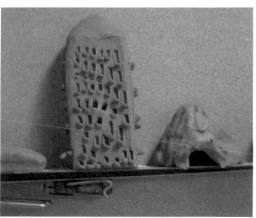

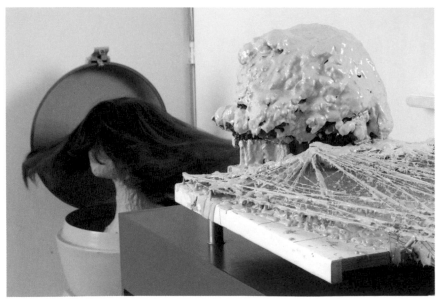

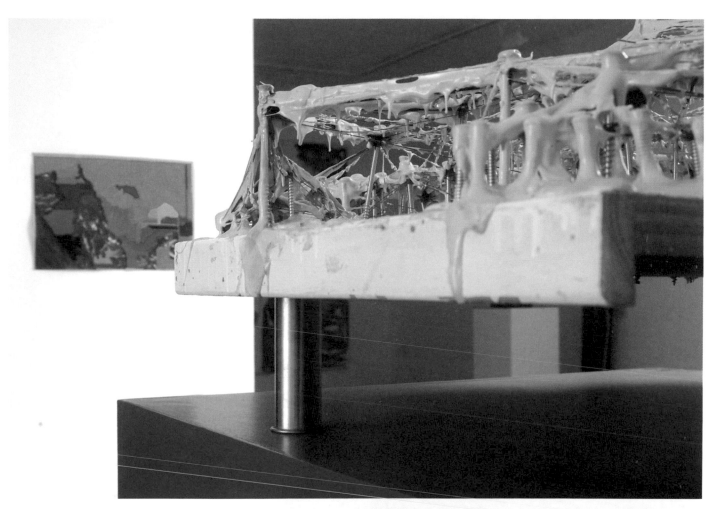

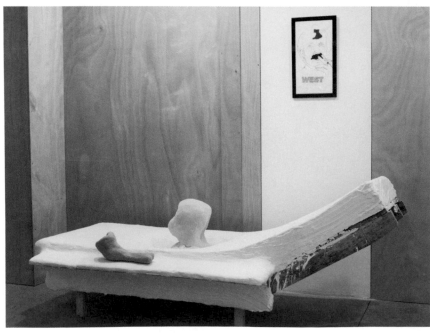

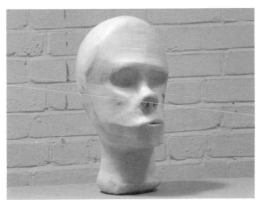

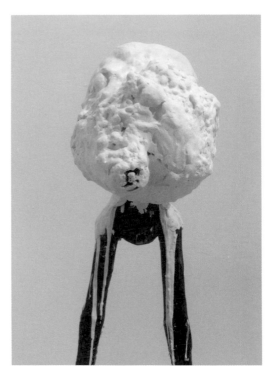

Wig shop / Head shop, 2005

INDEX
OF WORKS

HEADS

5 Soapstone, 300mm x 210mm x 240mm

6 Springstone, 180mm x 310mm x 160mm

7 Springstone, 180mm x 270mm x 150mm

8 Soapstone, 290mm x 350mm x 230mm

9 Springstone, 200mm x 450mm x 250mm

10 Soapstone, 200mm x 300mm x 270mm

11 Soapstone, 220mm x 330mm x 230mm

12 Soapstone, 240mm x 360mm x 260mm
Private Collection, London

13 Soapstone, 240mm x 420mm x 150mm

14 Soapstone, 230mm x 320mm x 190mm

15 Soapstone, 170mm x 390mm x 220mm

16 Soapstone, 230mm x 300mm x 240mm

17 Soapstone, 160mm x 270mm x 220mm

18 Springstone, 180mm x 240mm x 140mm

19 Springstone, 140mm x 280mm x 220mm

20 Springstone, 200mm x 400mm x 250mm

21 Springstone, 230mm x 450mm x 230mm

22 Soapstone, 200mm x 270mm x 160mm

23 Soapstone, 350mm x 440mm x 300mm

24 Limestone, 180mm x 480mm x 220mm

25 Soapstone, 230mm x 330mm x 170mm

26 Soapstone, 190mm x 180mm x 240mm

27 Soapstone, 420mm x 540mm x 140mm
Private Collection, London

28 Springstone, 160mm x 430mm x 270mm

29 Springstone, 150mm x 270mm x 170mm

30 Soapstone, 220mm x 330mm x 190mm

31 Soapstone, 180mm x 340mm x 220mm

32 Springstone, 190mm x 350mm x 220mm

33 Soapstone, 210mm x 330mm x 160mm

34 Soapstone, 180mm x 290mm x 220mm

35 Soapstone, 150mm x 340mm x 240mm

36 Soapstone, 240mm x 330mm x 200mm

37 Soapstone, 190mm x 300mm x 200mm

38 Soapstone, 340mm x 400mm x 240mm

39 Soapstone, 190mm x 280mm x 220mm

40 Soapstone, 420mm x 240mm x 270mm

41 Soapstone, 190mm x 230mm x 120mm

42 Limestone, 160mm x 250mm x 130mm

43 Limestone, 280mm x 320mm x 160mm

44 Soapstone, 200mm x 310mm x 200mm

45 Soapstone, 180mm x 290mm x 200mm

46 Springstone, 190mm x 290mm x 210mm

47 Springstone, 280mm x 330mm x 230mm

48 Springstone, 230mm x 500mm x 290mm

49 Springstone, 150mm x 420mm x 250mm

50 Springstone, 240mm x 350mm x 170mm

51 Springstone, 230mm x 330mm x 280mm

52 Springstone, 290mm x 180mm x 200mm

53 Soapstone, 130mm x 400mm x 250mm

54 Springstone, 160mm x 420mm x 270mm

55 Springstone, 160mm x 330mm x 210mm

56 Soapstone, 140mm x 290mm x 220mm

57 Soapstone, 200mm x 300mm x 220mm

58 Soapstone, 180mm x 320mm x 220mm

59 Soapstone, 220mm x 350mm x 210mm

60 Soapstone, 240mm x 310mm x 170mm

61 Soapstone, 160mm x 150mm x 130mm

62 Soapstone, 390mm x 240mm x 320mm
Freda and Izak Uziyel Collection

DRAWINGS

SELECTED WORKS

ISBN 978-0-9549119-2-8

Published to accompany the exhibitions:
Demos, 23 February – 21 April 2007
Northern Gallery for Contemporary Art, City Library and Arts Centre,
Fawcett Street, Sunderland SR1 1RE, www.ngca.co.uk
Heads, 13 July – 16 September 2007
Camden Arts Centre, Arkwright Road, London NW3 6DG
www.camdenartscentre.org

This publication is generously supported by Arts Council England,
North East and University of Sunderland.

The artist would like to thank:
Tali Cederbaum, Freda & Izak Uziyel, Dominic Benhura,
Alistair Robinson, Dean Turnbull & Alex Ryley at Northern Gallery
for Contemporary Art; Eric Bainbridge, Brian Thompson & Robert
Blackson at the University of Sunderland; Samantha Peace at
Arts Council England, North East; The Henry Moore Foundation;
Jenni Lomax & Bruce Haines at Camden Arts Centre; Ben Branagan,
Paulo Herkenhoff, Sacha Craddock; Stephen Wilson,
Pamela & Justin Silver; Suzy Shammah Gallery, Milan;
Givon Art Gallery, Tel Aviv.

All photography by Andy Keith except:
Colin Davison: p70
The artist: pp92-97, pp102-104
Ilya Melnikov: pp98-99
Yigal Pardo: pp100-101
Luigi Tricarico: p105
Rami Maymon: pp106-107

Graphic design & Art direction: Ben Branagan
Printed by Veenman Drukkers, The Netherlands